MILL
Pond

School

Boys & Girls

Infants

Mill Pond

Highest Point to which Ordinary Tide rises

B.M.
11·9

Saw Mill

M I L L   L A N

Rectory

·18

Grave Yard
(Disused)

Pump

B.M. 21·4

Vestry

15

St. Mary's Church
(Rectory)

Font

Seats for 750

Bear Inn

14

B.M. 15·

20

P.

Turk's Head Inn

C.R.

18

16.

The Creation of a Cathedral

The Story of St. Mary's, Truro

by

Fisher Barham

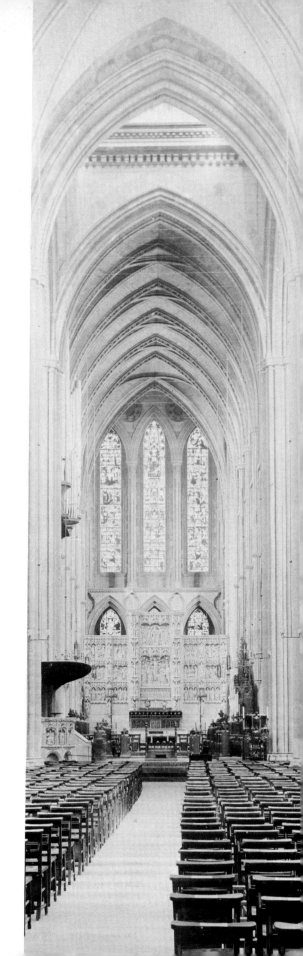

The cathedral from the air, showing how closely it is built into the city, much on the style of continental edifices. The Town clock, Boscawen Street, and other features are recognisable but changes have occured since the date of this photograph. The Post Office, designed by Sylvanus Trevail, has gone, and other buildings have been constructed on the inner ring road.

Contents

Foreword

The revival of the ancient diocese of Cornwall and the building of Truro Cathedral is a fascinating, imaginative and stirring story. As a Cornishman, with a great love for all things Cornish, Fisher Barham catches the creative spirit of the faith and Celtic fervour, which moved our Victorian founders, and their Edwardian successors, to recover the identity of the Church in Cornwall, and create the first great and beautiful Gothic cathedral to be built in England, since the Middle Ages. They accomplished all this at a time of deep depression when Cornish mining families were emigrating to all parts of the world in search of the livelihood denied them in their own country. Unlike the books we borrow from the library and read, or look at once, here is a book, all, who care about Cornwall, will want to possess. Fisher Barham has searched, far and wide, to produce a unique and absorbing collection of contemporary photographs, which bring to life a remarkable, yet comparatively short, period in the long history of Cornwall. There is a warmth in the author's narrative and selection of illustrations which, no doubt, springs from his own family's associations with the beginnings he now records for all time.

Henry Morgan Lloyd,
Dean of Truro.

My mother was a Truronian and, as most of my maternal relatives lived there, I naturally spent much of my childhood in the city. As a young boy my interests were in the movement of trains at the station or the ships in the river, the cathedral was just there, a part of the scene and a trifle awesome when close to. I vividly remember laying awake on a New Years Eve and hearing those same train whistles and ships hooters mingling with the glorious peals of the cathedral bells. I also remember, on one occasion, when very young, being taken to an evening service to hear the great Canon Lewis preach and being fascinated by his voice echoing from the sounding board then fitted over the pulpit.

In later years I became an amateur photographer and, with my camera, recorded many fine buildings, including cathedrals, in various parts of the country. I then came to realise the wonderful edifice almost at my own door. I have, during the last few years become a collector of old Cornish photographs and, in my researches, I have come across these splendid and unique records of the construction of Cornwall's cathedral. This has prompted me to take a new look at its splendours and its history and, I hope, through these pages that others may be encouraged to do the same, particularly as it approaches its centenary.

Fisher Barham

This water colour, by Frank Pearson in 1908, was his conception of the north aspect if his plans had been carried out to the full. It shows the line of the cloisters through to the cathedral school and the octagonal chapter house.

The architects general arrangement of his conception of the finished building. This shows there was little deviation from his original plans and this can be said of very few cathedrals in this country. Most were built over many years and different architects designed to their own style, also wars and pillage ruined many who were rebuilt in various forms. This drawing is also interesting because it affords a viewpoint which it is physically impossible to enjoy because of other buildings.

Preface

It is a not uncommon tendancy to suppose that any large and imposing church, of great architectural interest, should be a cathedral. In fact neither size, nor artistic merit have any bearing on the matter and, in theory, any church can be a cathedral. The one factor that makes it so, is that it contains the bishop's throne, or 'cathedra' and is thereby the mother church of the diocese. Naturally, in view of its importance and the need for facilities for administration and special services, a large edifice is usually chosen.

The founding of places of worship into cathedrals has been in three stages. At the time of the dissolution of the monasteries, by Henry VIII, there were seventeed cathedral churches in this country and, of these, nine were served by secular canons, that is priests who were not monks. These were at Chichester, Exeter, Hereford, Lichfield, Lincoln, London (St. Paul's), Salisbury, Wells and York and collectively they are known as the Cathedrals of the Old Foundation. Cathedral priories, which had been served by Benedictine monks were at Canterbury, Durham, Ely, Norwich, Rochester, Winchester and Worcester and these were now reorganised on secular lines as was that at Carlisle which had been under the Augustine order. At the same time, monastic churches at Bristol, Chester, Gloucester, Oxford, and Peterborough were elevated to cathedrals and all these, together with Westminster Abbey (the latter for a period of 10 years only) became the Cathedrals of the New Foundation.

After this no new sees were created for hundreds of years but changes in population began to create problems of administration. Some of the larger dioceses were split up and eventually, over several years, twenty new bishoprics were created which were established in the Cathedrals of the Modern Foundation. Of these, three were former monastic churches at St. Albans, Southwark and Southwell and fourteen others were former parish churches at Birmingham, Blackburn, Bradford, Bury, Chelmsford, Coventry, Derby, Leicester, Newcastle, Manchester, Portsmouth, Ripon, Sheffield and Wakefield. The remaining three were to be at Truro, Liverpool and Guildford and for these it was decided to build new cathedrals. The first to be constructed was at Truro and it is therefore unique in being a modern building but designed on gothic lines and what is more it is the first 'hand-built' cathedral of which there is a photographic record of the great work involved.

Overleaf: This magnificent and impressive view of Truro cathedral, was captured near sunset on a summers evening before a gathering storm, with the menacing blackness of the sky forming a backcloth for the gothic grandeur of the spires.

History

Little is known of the very early church in Cornwall but there is evidence of the existence of Cornish bishops in pre-Saxon times. The earliest names are not known with any certainty but we read of Petroc in the 6th century and the last of the truly Cornish bishops was Kenstec around 840 who made the first —unwilling — submission to Canterbury. The seat of these bishops is also vague with some reference to Bodmin and finally establishment at St. Germans. This seems to have been considered vulnerable to Viking invaders and it was moved to Crediton in 1027 and Cornwall lost its separate identity. In 1046 it was amalgamated with Exeter under Bishop Leofric and there it has remained to this day.

The bishops of Devon and Cornwall, and their staffs, had a difficult task administering to the needs of so large a territory and, over the years, as the population increased, this became more arduous. Letters and articles were put forward by many leading figures during the 19th century, both from the church and the laity, advocating the reinstatement of the Cornish bishopric, but with no success.

The visits to Cornwall of the bishop were infrequent and when he came he had much to do, particularly in conducting mass confirmations. On August 4th 1824, at St. Mary's church, between five and six hundred were received by him and the next day a further one hundred and forty. On August 9th 1842, Bishop Philpotts confirmed 400 schoolchildren when, at that time, he was recovering from an accident and had to be conveyed to the church in a sedan chair. He had long advocated the formation of a Cornish see and this experience must have influenced him to make a definite proposal that this should be done. His efforts resulted in Lord John Russell putting forward a bill for the creation of four new dioceses of which Cornwall should be one. This did not pass through parliament but a Royal Commission was appointed to investigate the matter thus shelving it for the time being. Meanwhile a healthy rivalry had grown up between Bodmin and Truro as to which should be the bishop's seat and this was further complicated when the commission's report was finally published. This certainly recommended a see for Cornwall but suggested St. Columb as it's base. This was due in some measure to Dr. Walker, vicar of St. Columb, who being wealthy, offered his vicarage (built at a cost of £7,000) and the avowson of the living estimated at £1,600 per annum. The Bishop of Exeter went along with this with £500 a year from his income (he would save that on travel anyway) plus his Cornish patronage. Lord Palmerston, the Prime Minister, however, turned down the whole idea in 1860 and refused to consider it further, adding that modern communications made it easier for the bishop to travel and visit his diocese. At that time, Henry of Exeter, was in his late eighties, in a wheel chair and he died in 1869. In 1863 a further petition had been presented from the Cornish Archdeaconry, to the Upper House of Convocation, pointing out the difficulties experienced and drawing attention to the quite different characteristics and needs of the Cornish and Devon peoples.

There was now another Prime Minister, Mr. Gladstone, and he appointed Dr. Temple as the new Bishop of Exeter. The latter was in favour of the idea of separation from the start, for his new diocese was now large in population as well as territory and he set about working for the restoration of the Cornish see. In 1875 a great public meeting, of all interested parties, was held in Plymouth, and from this a committee was formed and a deputation sent to the Prime Minister, now Dr. Disraeli, and this was led by Dr. Temple himself. They succeeded in principle and finance now became the critical factor. The bishop offered £800 plus his Cornish patronage, per annum, and a gift from Lady Rolle, practically set the seal on the matter. Other monies were promised and on August 17th 1876 the Act of Parliament was passed creating the Bishopric of Truro and just over twelve months later on August 17th city status was granted to Truro. The Order in Council stated that St. Mary's church should be the cathedral and the first bishop was named as Dr. E.W. Benson.

The First Bishop of Truro and his family.
Standing: Nellie Benson. Two canons of the Cathedral. Old servant Beth.
Seated centre: Mrs. Benson. Bishop Benson. Maggie Benson.
Seated front: Arthur Benson. "Watch". Hugh Benson. Fred Benson. Arthur died as a young man, Hugh became a Roman Catholic priest and the family servant, Beth, lived to be 92.

Edward White Benson was born in Birmingham on July 14th 1829. At the age of twenty four he became an assistant master at Rugby School and he was appointed headmaster of Wellington College when he was only twenty nine. After fifteen years in that post he was made Chancellor of Lincoln Cathedral and he was appointed to Truro, by the Queen in Letters Patent, gazetted on January 16th 1877. His new residence was the vicarage at Kenwyn, generously donated by the vicar, the Reverend R. Vautier, and it was given the Cornish name 'Lis Escop'. Dr. Benson was consecrated, as Bishop of Truro, in a ceremony at St. Paul's cathedral, London, on April 25th 1877, performed by the Archbishop of Canterbury, who was accompanied by the Bishops of London, Ely, Hereford, Lincoln, Salisbury, and Winchester. His enthronement at Truro took place shortly after on May 1st. On that day the clergy assembled at the Town Hall at 10.30 a.m. and were joined by the Mayors of Truro, Bodmin, Falmouth, Helston, Liskeard, Penryn, Penzance and Saltash, as this was a matter concerning the whole county. They all walked, in procession, to St. Mary's, now the cathedral, and were led by the Volunteers with their band. A most dignified service followed although there was little room in the old church for so large a gathering. After the ceremony they all returned to the council offices for lunch followed by speeches, and the band played selections to the crowd in Boscawen Street.

In olden days the people gathered at this spot to hear religious teachers and a tall cross was erected, hence the name High Cross to this part of Truro. St. Mary's church was rebuilt in the early part of the 16th century on the site of two former edifices and so this ground was concerned with spiritual teaching for many generations and hallowed by countless worshippers. The south east front, formed by the nave and south aisle, was richly decorated with carved stonework, but the later added, shorter, north aisle was less ornamental as were further additions in 1841. The steeple was erected in 1769, replacing a small bellcote, fitted with a single bell. The cost of this addition was £900 and it was in a quasi-classical style which was not a happy choice as it did not blend with the rest of the building. A clock and chimes, built by Richard Wills of Truro, were installed in 1760 but this had worn out and was replaced by the gift of another in 1851. The latter was removed at the church's demolition and later fitted in the campanile of the new cathedral. This bell tower and the retained south aisle are now the official parish church of Truro. Old St. Mary's measured 114 ft. in length, 38 ft. at it's greatest width and had an interior height of 24 ft.

The west front of old St. Mary's church with its rather severe classical style tower. The churchyard is more or less the site of the future nave.

The difficulties of operating as a cathedral from a small parish church were keenly felt and often expressed. The very first diocesan conference, held in the Truro Public Rooms, was addressed by, among others, Canon Philpotts, Archdeacon of Cornwall, and he made a strong speech advocating that something must be done. In subsequent discussion it was brought out that as the Order in Council named St. Mary's as the cathedral church, no other site could be considered without a further act of parliament, although some would have preferred a more dominant position, overlooking the town. A committee was then formed, under the chairmanship of the Earl of Mount Edgcumbe, to consider what steps to take. The first question was whether to enlarge the old church, and improve it's facilities, or to build a completely new structure. The Earl was of the latter view, and, as this was the bishop's greatest wish, it was agreed unanimously. Consideration was given to several names as the architect and the final choice was J.L. Pearson.

John Loughborough Pearson had designed many fine churches — St. Peter, Vauxhall. St. Augustines Kilburn, St. John's, Red Lion Square and many others including St. John's, Devoran, only five miles away. He was engaged in restoration work on Peterborough cathedral and later designed another cathedral on the other side of the world, at Brisbane, Australia, but this was not commenced until after his death. He had spent much time travelling and he absorbed some continental features in his ideas, hence the likeness of Truro to some edifices in Northern France. He estimated the costs for the building of the choir section to be £35,000, for the transepts, £20,000, and for the remainder of the main body £35,000, making a total of £95,000 although this did not include the cost of the three proposed towers.

This represented a vast sum in those days but with great faith they made their plans to proceed in the sure hope that it would be found. They already had £27,000 in hand, partly from appeals and partly from money which had been raised previously and set aside for the restoration of the old church. At once £10,000, of this fund, was spent acquiring land and for preparation work on the site. To take charge of this work and prepare the footings came the first Clerk of Works, James Bubb, a Londoner and a most devout and remarkable man who had been apprenticed to Pearson when he was twenty. A single man and non-drinker, he came, at the age of thirtyseven to devote the rest of his life in bringing to perfection the ideas of his mentor. During his surveys, of the ground and adjacent properties, he was often encumbered by curious onlookers and sometimes they became more hostile where he was contemplating the demolition of properties. He had abuse hurled at him on at least one occasion when he set up his theodolite in Old Bridge Street and stopped the traffic.

There was a desire, by the local committee, to use Cornish granite in the building but Pearson wanted Bath stone which gives a warmer look and is easier to fashion. James Bubb became the mediator between these two conflicting views and in collaboration with Colonel Cocks, of Treverbyn, he visited quarries all over the county and returned with samples of 72 varieties of stone. Eventually a compromise was reached with the exterior main walls of Cornish granite from Mabe and decorative dressings in Bath stone. The interior walling was of a softer variety of granite from St. Stephens and the columns and arches in the Bath stone. Other decorations were fabricated in serpentine, marble and other contrasting materials. In view of the later weathering the restriction in the use of the softer stone probably saved the cathedral from severe damage.

Bubb sometimes worked as much as 19 hours a day and had to contend with his employers demands, the interference of the (well meaning) local committee, the site conditions and some recalcitrant employees — a pretty tough lot in those days. In addition his health was deteriorating. He was in sole charge of the work until December 1881, when the first contractor was appointed and he was so pressurised that the two holes for the bases of the foundation stones were dug and filled with concrete only a few days before the formal ceremony took place.

The incorporation of the old south aisle of St. Mary's, presented the architect with many difficulties. Due to the lie of the ground and the creation of the crypt under the east end, the cathedral floor was considerably higher than the old church, also because of its proximity to the outer chancel wall, the usual support buttresses could not be provided but this was skilfully overcome. The strength for the outer wall was accomplished by an extra row of piers which, with their arches, converted the thrust downwards. This has resulted in a smaller aisle, or ambulatory, between St. Mary's and the south choir aisle and, as all three had different levels, a pleasing ascending effect up to the chancel is created, and the maze of soaring columns and arches have also produced an unusual and impressive

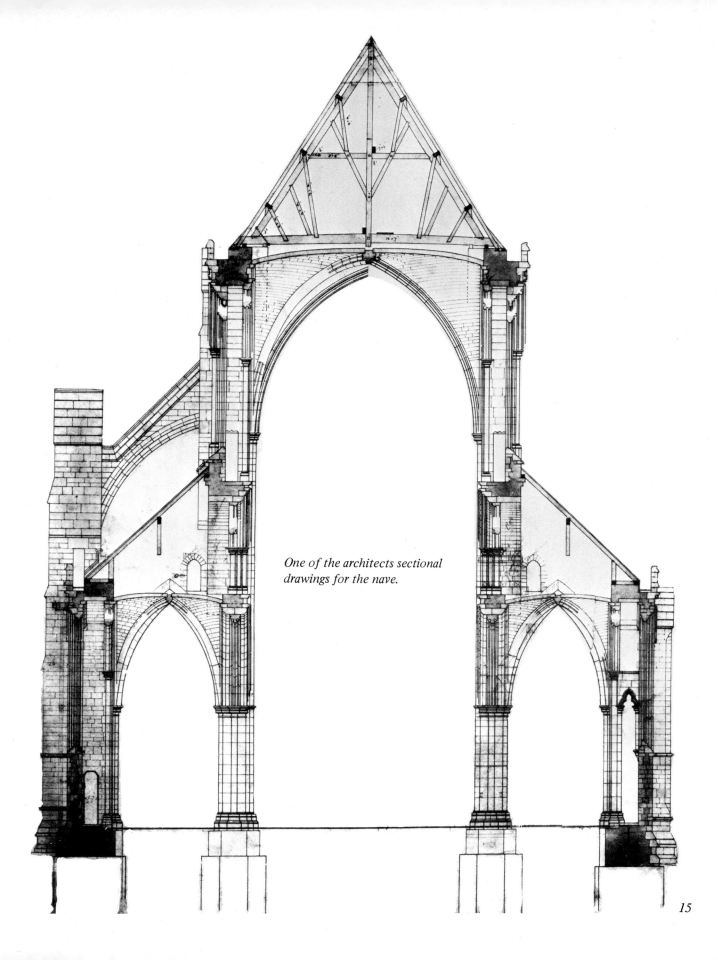

One of the architects sectional drawings for the nave.

15

vista. Within eighteen months of the plans being passed, all was ready for the official ceremony of laying the foundation stones. The reason for their being two to lay, is that the traditional position, in the north east would not allow room for the desired pomp and this was to be set in place in the presence of a select group. The second, or memorial stone was in the site of the old churchyard and was witnessed by a large assembly.

The great day was fixed for Thursday May 20th 1880 and was a most important one in the life of the church, the county, and indeed the whole country and Anglican church as it was the first new cathedral foundation stone to be laid since the Reformation, with the exception of the rebuilding of St. Paul's after the great fire. The event was blessed with fine weather and Truro made sure it was going to be a day to be remembered. The ceremony was to be performed by the Prince of Wales, Duke of Cornwall, later to become King Edward VII. He was accompanied by Princess Alexandra and their two sons, Prince Albert Edward, Duke of Clarence, and Prince George (later King George V) and the two lads captured all hearts in their sailor rigs. The Royal party came down, by train to Grampound Road station, where they were met by the Lord Lieutenant, The Earl of Mount Edgcumbe, and by Lord Falmouth, who was to be their host at his splendid home, Tregothnan, on the banks of the River Fal.

They set off, in an open carriage, passing through Probus, which was gaily decorated including a welcome arch of furze in bloom, a mass of yellow flowers. The little street with its fine church (the loftiest tower in Cornwall) was lined with folk and many farmers had assembled there on horseback. The Earl of Mount Edgcumbe was also ahorse and he marshalled them into an unofficial escort and they accompanied the carriage to the gates of Tregothnan, at Tresillian Bridge. This host of riders raised a terrific dust on the old dirt roads and soon looked like a company of millers. It was at this very spot, many years before, that the Cornish cavalry had surrendered in the Civil War.

On the evening of their arrival a splendid ball was held, in their honour, at the great house with everyone of note in the county attending and the Royal guests joining in until the early hours. The next day was one of rest for the Royal party, and they left, by boat, from the estate landing stage, for an excursion to beauty spots on the river. The great day followed and Truro had really gone to town (or should it be city) with a wealth of decorations which included no fewer than five triumphal arches. These were situated at Boscawen Bridge, Lemon Bridge, River Street, the cathedral entrance and also near Lander's monument in Lemon Street, all having been designed by a local man Sylvanus Trevail. Some 200 metropolitan policemen had been brought down from London to control the crowds, but there were no untoward incidents and, by all accounts, the men seemed to have enjoyed their visit which must have seemed like a journey to the ends of the earth for some of them in those days.

The Mayor, corporation and other local dignitaries assembled at the Town Hall at 11.30 a.m. Meanwhile the Prince and his party had left Tregothnan with an escort of 60 cyclists of the 1st Battalion, The Duke of Cornwall's Light Infantry, and they arrived at 11.35 a.m. After the customary loyal address the cortege passed up Lemon Street to the house Southleigh, which still stands, next to the Deanery. The Prince was the Grand Master of the Masons and a Grand Lodge was now opened in the dining room of the house, which had been laid out as a masonic temple. Meanwhile, in the Truro Assembly Rooms, The Provincial Grand Master, The Earl of Mount Edgcumbe, with a great gathering of masons, had opened a Provincial Grand Lodge. They then all walked, in reverse order of seniority, up Lemon Street, almost 600 strong, and with their banners making a most impressive sight. The carriage with the Princess and her sons now left Southleigh on the way to the church and the masons parted to let them through forming a guard of honour as they did so. The Prince and his retinue now emerged in their full colourful regalia and passed through the ranks of masons who fell in behind them. The splendid procession passed down the hill, through the masonic arch on Lemon Bridge and into Boscawen Street, through King Street, to the cathedral where other processions of clergy and civil authorities had assembled. The Mayor of Truro and Bishop Benson received the Princess and the Princes, conducted them to a dais and returned to the west to await the Prince. While all this activity was taking place the band of the Truro Volunteers was playing suitable music at High Cross. Finally the great Procession of masons with their Grand Master at it's head, arrived at the church. Various members of Grand Lodge were carrying the mallet, square, compass, plumb rule, columns, candlesticks and other masonic emblems while the Grand Chaplain, The Dean of York, carried a cushion, suspended by straps from his shoulders, on which was displayed an open bible.

Top Left:
The Welcome Arch at Boscawen Bridge with the Royal Carriage arriving from Tregothnan.
Top Right:
The arrival at the Town Hall.

Centre Left:
The Princess passing through the Royal Arch at the top of Lemon Street.
Centre Right:
The Gothic Arch at the entrance to the cathedral enclosure with the masons passing through.

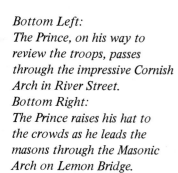

Bottom Left:
The Prince, on his way to review the troops, passes through the impressive Cornish Arch in River Street.
Bottom Right:
The Prince raises his hat to the crowds as he leads the masons through the Masonic Arch on Lemon Bridge.

'It is customary at the erection of all stately and superb edifices to lay the first, or foundation stone, at the north east corner on the building'. In this artist's impression from the GRAPHIC of May 29th 1880, H.R.H. Edward, Prince of Wales, is laying the foundation stone with masonic ritual.

The scene at the laying of the memorial stone on the nave site, with a great number of masons present and the stands erected for the ceremony.

The north east foundation stone under which were deposited coins and relevant documents.

TO THE GLORY OF GOD
THE CORNER-STONE OF THIS CATHEDRAL CHURCH
OF ST MARY IN TRURO, WAS PLACED BY
H.R.H. ALBERT EDWARD, PRINCE OF WALES AND DUKE OF CORNWALL,
GRAND MASTER OF THE ANCIENT FREE
AND ACCEPTED MASONS OF ENGLAND,
THURSDAY THE 20TH DAY OF MAY, A.D. 1880.

TO THE GLORY OF GOD
THIS STONE WAS PLACED BY
H.R.H. ALBERT EDWARD
PRINCE OF WALES
AND DUKE OF CORNWALL,
ON THE SAME DAY
AS THE N.E. CORNER-STONE
OF THIS CATHEDRAL CHURCH
20TH MAY, A.D. 1880.

The memorial stone set in the nave pillar and fashioned in granite.

The Prince was received by the Bishop and at that moment a Royal Salute was fired and the band struck up the National Anthem. At noon the great service began with singing by the choir and prayers by the Bishop. The official party proceeded to the east and there His Royal Highness laid the Foundation Stone, testing it with the square, level and plumb rule, according to ancient custom. The ritual of scattering corn, pouring oil and sprinkling wine, over the stone followed, in accordance with masonic rites at the establishment of a new temple. The Prince and the clergy then proceeded to the west while the Princess, and her sons were accommodated in a stand overlooking the splendid scene in the old churchyard. On each side of the ground, where it was hoped the nave would later rise, stands had been erected, now thronged with people, and in the space between was the great body of the masons. The memorial stone, now laid by the Prince, was part of the base of one of the future pillars of the nave and was in granite as it would remain in the open, exposed to the elements for many years. When the cathedral was later completed this column was carried up to the arch in this same stone and is the only pillar of this material in the church.

After the Benediction the procession returned to the Market House, which had been gaily decorated and where lunch was now served with many speeches to follow. After these were concluded the Prince rode, on horseback, to Treliske, where the Volunteers and Militia were drawn up to be reviewed. On the route His Royal Highness passed through cheering crowds and at one point he was greeted by the strains of 'God Bless the Prince of Wales' played by a circus band seated on a golden trailer and drawn by an elephant. During the civic lunch the musical background had been provided by the string band of the Royal Marines and in the evening a concert was given, in the cathedral enclosure by the band of the 15th Regiment, The King's Own Borderers. The day's events concluded with a firework display from across the river at Poltisko, presented by a Mr. Pain of London, a name to be associated with such shows for many years to come. On the following Sunday there was an open air service, at the cathedral nave site with Bishop Benson standing by the granite column to preach his sermon and the congregation accommodated in the stands erected for the ceremony. Folk had walked long distances to attend and it was estimated 4,000 were present. It was a most impressive service with the singing led by just four cornets.

James Bubb now took over the church and just four months later it was closed. On the Sunday before there was another great congregation assembled, with many standing at the doors. Early on the Monday morning 100 people took communion and there followed a wedding between Joseph Cock of Truro and Emily Dyer of Perranzabuloe and as they left the building the workmen moved in to begin demolition. As there would be no place of worship for some years, a temporary wooden building was erected, on the nave site (see page 87) and this was furnished with many of the fitments from the old church. It cost £430 to erect, seated 400 and had the reputation of being excessively cold in winter and hot in summer. It was only intended to last about 7 years but it did better than that. After fulfilling its purpose at Truro it was sold to a firm who erected it at Drump Road Redruth as the 'Cathedral Boot Works' and after many changes of ownership, there it stands to this day with it's wood gothic style windows still recognisable. It must have been one of the strangest buildings ever to rank as a cathedral.

Hoardings were now placed around the site and the foundations were excavated, the crypt constructed followed by the lower courses of the walls and columns. Now, unhappily, after two years, ill health and his hard unstinting work finally broke poor Bubb and he died on May 17th 1882, at the age of thirty nine. He had done so much to ensure the perfection of his task that he had worn himself out and then contracted typhoid. He had received praise from all quarters including congratulations from the Prince, as His Royal Highness phrased it 'From one mason to another'.

"On May 20th 1882, two years after (the foundation ceremony) almost to the very hour, his mortal remains were brought forth from the darkened chamber, after the cathedral choristers standing surpliced, within the shadow of the northern buttress of the new edifice, had sung sweet music over his corpse, the tearful hundred odd artificers carried, in turn, their beloved chief to the cemetery. Nearly a score of local dignitaries, marshalled by the Lord Bishop and followed by an immense crowd of citizens, went mournfully as well. At the grave the funeral service was read jointly by Canons Mason and Harvey and Chancellor Whittaker, after which the benediction was pronounced by His Lordship. Then the Bishop of Truro, arrayed as he was in full canonicals, went to the bereaved and venerable sire and the weeping sisters, at the open graveside, of the good man who was gone and alternately grasping each affectionately by the hand, bid them in Jesus name be comforted. It was at this moment that the whole graveyard wept". Such was the very vivid and dramatic reporting in those days.

The new clerk of works was Robert Swain and he remained until the choir and transepts were completed and the cathedral consecrated. There were constant worries about raising the necessary money and each stage of the construction seemed in jeopardy. When the choir section was almost finished a start was made on the south transept and for a time it was thought a temporary cover would have to be built over this part but at last the cash was found and the north transept added. Another crisis followed when Mr. Pearson insisted that two bays of the nave must be partially built to counteract the thrust of the central crossing arch and again the money was found. So, at the end of seven years, the first great stage of this inspired vision was finished. As a permanent reminder of the old church which had served as his cathedral, the Bishop had the top of the spire and the weather vane, from old St. Mary's, erected in the garden at Lis Escop.

In 1882, when the Archbishop of Canterbury died, Dr. Benson was invited, by the Queen, to fill the office and he gladly accepted. He left Truro in January 1883 and was succeeded by Dr. Wilkinson, Rector of St. Peters, Eaton Square who had been associated with Truro cathedral as one of the examining chaplains.

Looking over the river to Truro from the high ground at Poltisko. Taken around 1877, it shows old St. Mary's church rising from the centre of the town.

The first stage in the building with the crypt under construction.

The completed crypt, which did duty as the chapter house for many years.

The main work starts on building the cathedral with the commencement of the choir in June 1882.

Progress on the same spot with St. Mary's aisle rebuilding on the right. October 1882.

The maze of columns begins t rise in April 1883. The small ambulatory is already recognisable and the South window of St. Mary's aisle.

In July 1883 the choir begins to take shape while masons prepare further stones.

24

From the south east, in January 1883, with the rebuilding of St. Mary's aisle in the foreground.

In November, 1883, less than a year later when viewed from the same position considerable progress has been made.

25

Seen from the west, in January 1884, the main choir approaches completion.

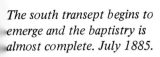

The south transept begins to emerge and the baptistry is almost complete. July 1885.

In January 1886 both the transepts are now well advanced.

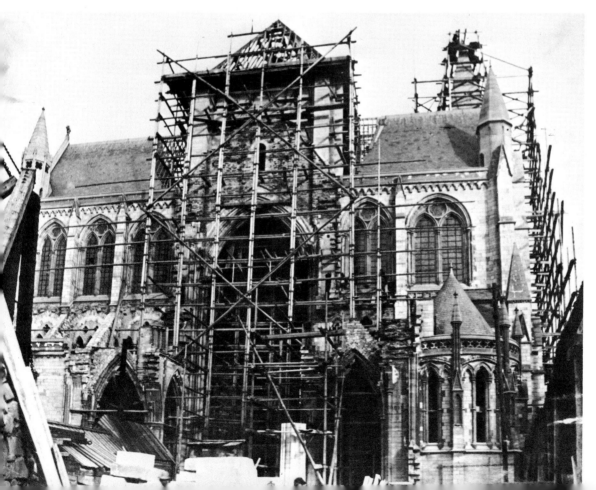

Choir, transepts and baptistry almost complete in March 1887. The great arch at the crossing will now be temporarily bricked over.

Over the roofs, of cathedral lane, we see the choir in October 1884.

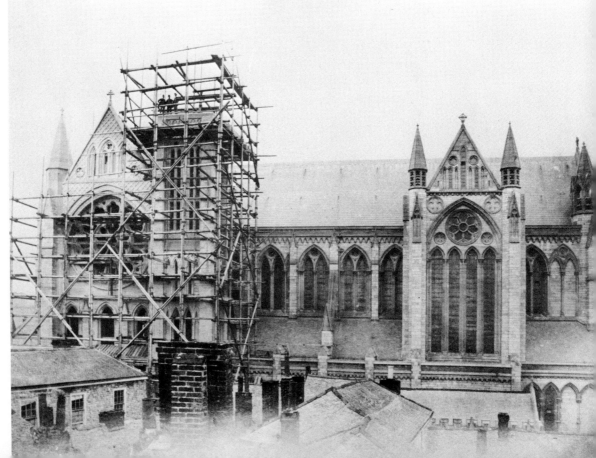

From the same position in July 1886, we see the transepts have been added, and the clock tower is under construction.

28

This tranquil view, from the north, sees the cathedral as it was in 1887, the choir and transepts, reflected in the quiet waters of the mill pool, a part of the River Allen.

Seven years after the foundation stones were laid, the new edifice was ready for the service of consecration and now consisted of the choir, transepts, St. Mary's aisle and two bays of the nave with a blanked off wall which for some years the clergy would have to face when conducting the services. At this stage the square base of the central tower, up to roof level, was also built and capped.

For the great day it was hoped the Queen might be able to attend but it was felt the long journey would be too much for her especially after recent events. Once again the Prince of Wales came to Truro to represent her. This time the occasion was of a more religious nature but the city was again gaily decorated and in festive mood. It was November 3rd 1887 and a very blustery day with storms the night before which threatened to wreck the flags and bunting. The day before, the Prince had laid the foundation stone of All Saint's church, Falmouth, and he had spent the night on the Royal yacht Osborne, in the harbour and had, no doubt, felt the storm. He came up to Truro by train and was once again greeted by the Earl of Mount Edgcumbe. After inspecting the Guard of Honour, mounted by a company of the Truro Volunteer Battalion D.C.L.I., with their band, he entered his carriage and, with a mounted escort, drove into the city, by a roundabout route, Green Lane, Lemon Street, Boscawen Street and King Street. The way was lined by 400 of the County Volunteers, 120 County Police and 28 Marines, presumably from the Osborne, with another company of the Volunteers as Guard of Honour at the cathedral. Lemon Street was impressively lined with 80 men on horseback.

Inside the building, the body of the church was soon filled with persons connected with the work of the diocese and the town. Admission was by ballot and there were some 2,500 on the floor of the church with others accommodated in temporary galleries erected over the incomplete two bays of the nave. Still others were in the triforium including the workmen who had built the edifice and were now to see it come to life.

At 10.30 a.m. from the wooden building which had served as a cathedral for seven years, came a great company of the clergy of the diocese and they formed into two columns and entered the building, passing down each side of the choir. Then from outside could be heard the singing of the ancient hymn 'Urbs Beata', by the procession of the choir and the bishops, who had robed in the crypt and now passed around the east and the south to approach the west entrance. They were led by the bandsmen of the Royal Marines and the order of the procession was thus:

Cross Bearer (and attendants)
Musicians   (in pairs)
Choristers   (in pairs)
Lay Vicars and Vicars Choral   (in pairs)
Preceptors of the cathedral and St. Peters, Eaton Square
Diocesan Inspector and Vice Chancellor of the cathedral
Rural Deans of the Diocese   (in pairs)
Prebendaries of St. Endellion   (in pairs)
Honorary Canons of other cathedrals   (in pairs)
Prebendaries of Exeter   (in pairs)
Canons Residentiary of other cathedrals (in pairs)
Archdeacons
The Dean of Exeter
Canons of Truro   (in pairs)
Archdeacons of Truro diocese   (in pairs)
Bishops (in pairs, each attended by his chaplain)
The Registrar of the diocese and the Architect

The Pastoral Staff (Borne by the Bishop's Private Chaplain)
The Lord Bishop of the Diocese, Dr. Wilkinson
Chaplains   (in pairs)
The Apparitor General of the Province
The Mace Bearer
The Archbishop's Cross (Borne by His Grace's Domestic Chaplain)
The Lord Archbishop of Canterbury, Dr. Benson
Train Bearers
Chaplains
Provincial Registrar.

The bishops, in the procession, were those of, Argyl & The Isles & Aberdeen, Bedford, Nottingham, Colchester, Trinidad, Ely, Salisbury, Exeter, Southwell, Newcastle, Lichfield, St. Asaph, Bath & Wells, Bangor, Winchester, London, and Bishops Mitchison and Blyth of Jerusalem.

At the west end they were joined by the Mayor & Corporation of Truro to await the arrival of His Royal Highness. After he was greeted the Bishop led them, through the ranks of choristers to the door of the cathedral (a temporary one in the uncompleted nave) on which he gave the customary knocks with his staff, saying "Lift up your heads, O ye gates", and this was repeated by the choir. From within, the clerks replied, "Who is the King of Glory". and the Bishop replied, "The Lord of Hosts". The door was then thrown open by Robert Swain, Clerk of Works, and the procession entered. As they reached their positions at the steps of the choir, a most colourful scene emerged. Ranged there were the nineteen bishops from home and overseas, in their brilliant robes, the Mayor in fur trimmed scarlet, the Naval and Military Officers and the sombre black and white of the clergy.

Then began the solemn service of the Consecration with the Bishop, and His retinue, passing around the various parts of the cathedral — The Font, The Pulpit, The Lectern, The Place of Marriage (Chapel steps) and the Sanctuary, each in turn being hallowed, with the organist playing appropriate music between each intonation. The Venerable W.J. Philpotts, Archdeacon of Cornwall, then read the Sentence of Consecration from the altar and it was then signed by the Bishop and witnessed by the Prince of Wales. There followed the Communion after which Dr. Benson Archbishop of Canterbury gave the first sermon from the pulpit of the church he had worked so hard to create.

At the conclusion of the four hour service there was a grand civic banquet at the Concert Hall attended by over 500 of the leading figures in the county and their wives. There was a musical background on the organ and the splendid, mouth watering menu included: Boars Head, Galantine of Turkey, Galantine of Chicken, Ornamented Tongue, Roast Chicken, Roast Pheasant, Partridges, Lobster Salads, Fillets of Sole in Aspic, Oysters in Aspic and to follow, Trifle Maraschino Jelly, Meringue de Venice, Charlotte Russe, Italian Cream, Macedoine of Fruit, Gateau a la Royal. After the conclusion of the speeches which followed the Prince drove through the streets again, on his way to the station, but by now the rain was falling and this damped the crowds enthusiasm. There was an evensong at 4 p.m. with the Bishop of London giving the address and there was a service of praise at 7.30 p.m. to enable as many as possible to join in worship in the new cathedral of it's first day. At all these services there was splendid singing by the choir which had been augmented by choristers from the cathedrals of St. Paul's, Bristol, Exeter, Gloucester, Hereford, Lichfield, Wells, Oxford and also St. Peter's, Eaton Square, because of it's association with Dr. Wilkinson. There were also musical concerts for the general public in the afternoon and evening in the Public Rooms and later the city was illuminated (by gas!). A Grand Reception was given in the evening by the Mayor and Mayoress of Truro to crown this great day.

Commemoration pages from the Illustrated London News of November 12th 1887, after the consecration.

EAST VIEW FROM NEW BRIDGE

The interior of the choir and the windows under scaffold during the building.

From the site of the future nave we see the church at the time of its consecration with the base of the central tower capped and the two bays of the nave covered and blanked off. It remained in this state for the next nine years.

An early stage in the construction of the nave showing the hefty timber built hoist and the first courses of the main walls.

As the nave rises higher the west end begins to take shape and the cobbled streets of Truro are clearly seen.

This splendid photograph of the emergence of the west front and porch, clearly shows the accuracy and precision of the timber pole scaffolding. In the foreground are several of the horse buses which ran to other towns and villages from this departure point at High Cross.

The nave virtually complete and surmounted by it's stone cross which was added with some small ceremony. The great west window has appeared and the bases of the western towers are seen although these were not added until some years later and this was taken about 1902.

A total of £19,000 had now been raised for the building and establishment of the great church and there now followed a period of consolidation when, for a span of nine years, no further construction took place. Truro's first bishop, Dr. Benson, now Archbishop of Canterbury, died in October 1896 and it was felt that the church should be completed as a fitting memorial to his work. Although there was a lack of funds, the treasurer of the cathedral, Mr. A.P. Nix, cut the first sod on May 20th 1898 and a start was made in the following January in the hope that the necessary money would be found. The architect, J.L. Pearson, had died in the intervening years and his son Frank Pearson took over the work, using his father's plans. There was also a new bishop, Dr. Gott, the third in line, as Dr. Wilkinson had retired through ill health although he later recovered and eventually became Primus of Scotland.

With the construction of the nave we encounter the 'twist' in the ground plan of the building. The choir had followed the line of old St. Mary's church to incorporate the aisle but had this line continued the west end would have been in the middle of the street as the roadway takes a turn. A six foot deviation was built in and this was camouflaged in the first bays of the nave. This stage of the building was completed in five years and the ceremony of the Benediction of the Nave took place on July 15th 1903. Once again this was a great day of rejoicing and blessed with the presence of the Duke and Duchess of Cornwall but this time, as Edward had ascended the throne, it was their Royal Highnesses George and May, later to become the beloved King George V and Queen Mary.

Truro had made great preparations and had spent £650 to erect decorations, provide the bands, the civic lunch and the firework display. Once again the Royal Party were to stay at Tregothnan, the home of Lord Falmouth, and as before they came by train to Grampound Road. The little country station, now alas no longer in use, was smothered in ferns and other local plants. The Royal couple were met by their host and the High Sheriff of Cornwall, Mr. P.D. Williams of Caerhayes and here we see the march of progress as, instead of horse carriages the Cornishmen had arrived in their motor cars. Mr. Williams was driving his splendid new Wolseley and as an interesting sidelight, the registration number later carried on this car — AF 25 — is still carried on the Williams family cars.

At the station the musical welcome came from the St. Stephens brass band and on the journey to Tregothnan the Royal carriage was escorted by four policemen on cycles. Many members of the public also followed on their bicycles forming an unofficial escort rather like the farmers had escorted the Prince's father in 1880.

The next morning, Thursday, several carriages left Tregothnan and in the last of these were the Royal couple, with an escort of cyclists of the 1st Battalion of the Cornwall Rifle Volunteers. Many people had come out from Truro to meet them and from Union Hill onwards the way was lined with folk and the official decorations began at St. Paul's church. At the Town Hall, the Mayor met them and gave the customary address of welcome after which the Prince and Princess retired to a room in the council chambers. A civic procession then formed up and made it's way to the cathedral. Some 300 people were already seated in the church and at the door, awaiting the Royal party, were the Bishop of Truro, The Archbishop of Canterbury (Dr. Davidson) and twenty seven other bishops from home and overseas. The main body of the clergy walked into the cathedral preceeded by four trumpeters and the choristers of Truro and Exeter. The Prince and Princess were met and escorted to their seats and the great service began. As the cathedral had already been consecrated this was a service of benediction at the completion of the nave and main body of the church. Once again there followed the great civic banquet at the Market Hall with some 500 seated. There were many splendid speeches and in his reply the Prince of Wales read a message, from his father, which included the words ". . . My great satisfaction that you should finish the work which I commenced". This was an amusing reference to his having laid the foundation stones over 23 years previously.

During the lunch the string band of the Royal Marines played selections and throughout the day various band concerts were given for the public's enjoyment. The Artillery Volunteers had played in the Victoria Gardens in the afternoon, The Rifle Volunteers had played at the cathedral square at 3 p.m., at Landers Monument at 6 p.m. and in Boscawen Street at 8 p.m. At Tremorvah the crowd was entertained by the band of H.M.S. Vivid. During the day the routes had been held by some 2,500 men, drawn from the Cornwall & Devon Miners Artillery, The Royal Cornwall Rangers and The Rifle Volunteers. The Royal party passed through their ranks while driving around the city before departing for Tregothnan. In the afternoon the Bishop and Mrs. Gott gave a garden party at Lis Escop and 1,400 people attended. There was an evensong at the cathedral for 6 p.m. and the great day was once again ended with a firework display, this time at Tremorvah.

The scene at the arrival at Grampound Road station. The Prince and Princess are seated in the carriage while Lord Falmouth enters.

During the drive around Truro, the Royal carriage descends, through the cutting in Richmond Hill, escorted by the Volunteers, with their bush hats rather reminiscent of the Anzacs.

The procession of the clergy with Bishop Gott in the fine ceremonial cloak which the chapter still have. The men and boys seem oblivious to the fact that they are almost rubbing shoulders with the Archbishop of Canterbury, Dr. Davidson.

The Bishop approaches the west door, preceded by his cross. The lack of dignity in the lines of troops is noticeable but of course these are not regulars.

As an interesting sidelight to these events the Royal visitors stayed in the Duchy until the following Monday and were taken touring, by motorcar, visiting Bodmin, Lanhydrock, Restormal, Helston and the Lizard. Due to the uncertainty of starting their early motors, in most cases they passed through places at a fair pace so as not to stall. In Perranarworthal a youngster had to be carried, at a fast trot to keep up with the Royal car in order to present a bouquet. They also opened Poldhu experimental wireless station, being escorted by Signor Marconi himself. It may well be said that these few days in the county by the Royal Party had some influence on the beginnings of the great tourist industry of Cornwall. On Monday they went down the river to Falmouth and laid the commemoration stone of the Prince of Wales pier and toured the town before leaving by train for London.

The Prince of Wales (George V) lays the foundation stone of the Prince of Wales Pier, Falmouth, watched by the unmistakable figure of Princess May (Queen Mary). Above the stone, on the crane can be seen a lad with an early box camera and off Trefusis Point are old warships of the training squadron.

The beginning of the great central tower. The temporary capping has been removed and the first part of the maze of staging is in place. The nave is still incomplete in this view from the north east in 1902.

Seen from the south west, the central tower has now almost risen to the base of the spire.

44

A close up, from the northwest, showing the intricate scaffolding as the tower climbs skywards, also the tall timber hoist from the stone masons yard.

Although still covered in a timber case, the spire can be seen to be almost complete.

From High Cross the clean stonework of the new cathedral is seen to advantage and the central tower is almost completed.

From over the river, in New Bridge Street, generally accepted as the finest viewpoint of the cathedral, the completed tower is emerging from its chrysalis case to show its beauty.

The top of the headgear of the hoist used to bring up materials from the stoneyard, in the precinct, for building the central tower. The small railway ran across a bridge to the base of the tower staging.

The appearance of the cathedral, from the north east in 1905, with the central tower only completed.

The massive tower, the central feature of the cathedral, was still under construction when the nave was completed and it could not be included in the general benediction. Six months later the top stone was added by Mr. Dennis and shortly after there followed another ceremony and service. The cost of the structure, £15,000 had been donated by the father of the above Mr. Dennis and during the occasion he officially handed over the tower to the Earl of Mount Edgcumbe with these words:

"My Lord, I request, that you receive this tower and spire, built in testimony and thankful remembrance felt by the County of Cornwall, for Her Majesty, Queen Victoria and the blessings of her reign, to be called by her name, in order to present it to the Bishop, to be by him, offered and blessed to the Glory of God and the service of His Holy Church".

There followed a short voluntary by the organist and, as he played, a screen, which had hitherto covered the base of the tower, was drawn aside to reveal its inner height and beauty in a most impressive manner. There is a carving, in one of the stone piers of the tower, on the nave side, which records that it was the gift of James Hawke Dennis, a Cornishman.

There were opinions expressed that the design of the central tower was not compatible with the rest of the building, being too heavy. The western towers have a slim, soaring effect whereas the Victoria tower appears bulky, but it certainly contributes to the continental appearance of the cathedral. The height from the floor to the weather vane is 244 ft. and there is a popular fallacy that this represents the distance, in miles, to London, but this is a trifle short of the necessary 280.

The two western towers under construction, seen from the mill pool. Note the men on the top platforms and how these stagings give the towers a 'mortar board' appearance.

Looking over the parapet of the newly completed cathedral school, another view of the work proceeding on the two towers.

From street level at High Cross we see the mass of scaffold encasing the ascending twin towers.

There now only remained the two western towers to complete the main body of the church and work was now concentrated on these, their cost of £20,000 having been donated by Mrs. Hawkins of Trewinnard in memory of her husband. They were completed in 1910 and special services were held on the Monday and Tuesday, June 20th, and 21st. For these occasions the Truro choir was augmented by that of Exeter and their organist, Dr. Wood, and the Truro organist, Dr. Monk, alternated at the console or conducting. On the Monday there was a choral evensong and on the Tuesday morning a choral communion. For the main service of Benediction admission was by ticket only and the cathedral was full. The celebrations were intended to be held in May but the death of Edward VII, who had been so much associated with the cathedral, caused the postponement.

The Mayors of Truro, Penzance, Liskeard, St. Ives and Bodmin attended and fifty seats had been set aside for the Freemasons, who attended in full regalia, and were drawn mainly, from those who had been present at the foundation stone laying. The procession of the clergy entered the building and the proceedings began at noon. Mrs. Hawkins formally handed over the towers to the Bishop, who was now Dr. William Stubbs, the fourth to hold the office during the cathedral's construction. After a short peal on the bells, which were also handed over and included in the general benediction, the Bishop preached a sermon. At the conclusion of the service there was the celebration lunch given by Bishop and Mrs. Stubbs and attended by 100 guests. Following the service a programme of bell ringing commenced with teams from the west country and a Cornish band whose photograph appears on page 59. There was change ringing, with short breaks, between 3 and 6.50 p.m. The two new towers, perhaps the most graceful external features of the church, were the North east, named the King Edward VII and the South east, named the Queen Alexandra. They were practically identical except that the King Edward tower houses the bells and has a floor for the ringers which shortens the main lancets and there are also minor differences in the pinnacles and small lancets around the spires.

So in just thirty years from laying the foundation stones, the cathedral was completed and during nine of those years no construction was taking place. The main external walls were of granite with dressings of Bath stone and it is one of the few cathedrals which were executed exactly as planned and it has not suffered the additions, alterations and 'improvements' that many older edifices have undergone. The only deviation from the architects design is on the north side, here, around a small close, it was intended to have a square precinct surrounded on three sides by a cloistered walk and the main fabric was left in an 'open' state to facilitate the connections. The first great war stopped the construction at that time and it was not until 1935 that the first bay was built. From a door, in the north transept, a flight of stone stairs led down to the ground where there had previously been a wooden hut and timber stairs. The Cornish freemasons subscribed to a fund for this cloister bay as a memorial to the part they, and their Grand Master, The Prince of Wales, had played at the laying of the foundation stones, just over 50 years previously.

On the occasion of their annual service, on July 28th 1935, a Provincial Grand Lodge was opened in the Regent Theatre (City Hall) Truro, and afterwards they walked in full regalia, to the close of the cathedral. In the retinue were four young boys, sons of masons, attired in surplices and wearing mortar boards, carrying between them on a cushion, the Volume of the Sacred Law — The Holy Scriptures. When the company reached the cloister there was a ceremony and the Provincial Grand Master, Lord St. Levan, handed over the new addition to the church with these words:

"On behalf of the Freemasons of Cornwall we commend to the care of the Dean and Chapter, this stairway and cloister bay, which are offered to the Glory of God the Most High and for use in the service of the Cathedral Church."

The freemasons then passed up the stairs, through the transept door and into the cathedral for their service, and Bishop Hunkin, himself a Truro man and a member of the craft, preached the sermon. The second great war stopped further progress on the cloisters and afterwards it was found that the increasing costs of building them on gothic lines laid down by the architect was prohibitive and no further bays were built or are contemplated at present or in the foreseeable future.

The north side of the cathedral with the original wood hut entrance to the north transept.

The four young sons of masons, carrying the Holy Scripture, in the procession.

*The cloister today with the
stonework capped although
some future alteration may be
made.*

*The cloister bay, as it appeared
at the time it was completed,
with the stonework left in an
'open' state.*

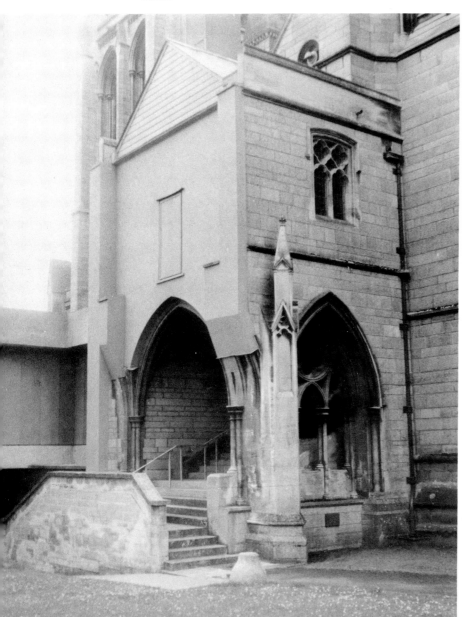

Some of the men engaged on the building of the choir around 1883. The number employed varied according to the work in hand but never seems to have exceeded 110 men. It was often arduous and very exposed working at height especially during the winter months. A rest room was provided and the public was asked to donate books and magazines. In general it is apparent that the workmen took a pride in their work and in being involved in the construction of such a wonderful and unique church. At first the Bishop conducted prayers each morning with the men but later a weekly supplication was considered sufficient and less of an interruption.

Despite the dangers involved only one serious accident occured in the whole of the building work and this was very near the completion. During the erection of the two western towers a steam hauled lift cage was in use to transport men and materials to the top and when it reached it's summit it was lowered on to safety catches. On one occasion this precaution was not taken and at one o'clock the men coming off work jumped into the cage which with their weight immediately ran away down the shaft a distance of some 70 ft. It was slowed a little by the brake drag but it hit the bottom with great force. Just before the impact one man, E. Rowe leapt out and escaped with a bad shaking and another W. Whitford only sustained bad bruising but the other four were taken to hospital. George Williams had a sprained ankle, Fred Ford a dislocated foot and George Richardson had a broken thigh and crushed foot. The worst injuries were to the last man, Richard Granville, who, apart from face abrasions and a broken thigh, had such damage to his lower limbs that one foot was amputated at once and the other a few days later.

He received £300 in compensation as he could not work again but he lived on with artificial legs, until he was 76 and his picture appears on the 'TOM TROT' confectionary tin made by the Truro firm of Furniss & Co. The contractors for the choir and transepts were Messrs. Shillitoe of Bury St. Edmunds and for the nave and tower they were Messrs. Willcocks of Wolverhampton and both employed some local and itinerant labour.

A close up of the building of the doorway surrounds for the west porch. The careful scaffold erection is noticeable and more of the workmen, none without a hat.

The Bells

Treble	Saints Mary & Nicholas	2ft 5½in diam.	E	6cwt 1qr 19lbs	£40.19s.
2	Saint Kea	2ft 6 5/8in diam.	D	6cwt 3qr 17lbs	£44.2s.
3	Saint Piran	2ft 8 5/8in diam.	C	7cwt 2qr 17lbs	£48.16s.6d.
4	Saint Petroc	2ft 9½in diam.	B	7cwt 3qr 26lbs	£51.19s.6d.
5	Saint Germans	3ft 0¼in diam.	A	8cwt 3qr 9lbs	£56.14s.
6	Saint Nectan	3ft 3in diam.	G	10cwt 3qr 16lb	£72.9s.
7	Saint Agnes	3ft 7½in diam.	F	14cwt 1qr 12lb	£100.16s.
8	Saint Kenwyn	3ft 10½in diam.	E	18cwt 1qr 18lb	£119.14s.
9	Saints Madron & Gulval	4ft 3 3/8in diam.	D	23cwt 3qr 4lb	£157.10s.
Tenor	Saints Probus & Grace	4ft 9 5/8in diam.	C	33cwt 3qr 10lb	£220.10s.

Total weight with apparatus 7¼ tons.

The bells were paid for by various benefactors and bodies and were cast at the Loughborough Foundry of Messrs. Taylors who are still engaged in the same trade. They were fitted with the Ellacombe chiming apparatus which was a gift of the pupils and staff, past and present of Probus School which no longer exists.

Total cost of bells and chiming gear was £1550.

The Cornish Band of Bellringers.

Back Row. (l. to r.)	* W. H. Sleeman	Kenwyn
	* B. Williams	St. Stephens in Brannel
	* J. Creba	
	E. T. Price	Clerk of the Works
	H. Bentley	Bell Hanger. Messrs. Taylors
	A. P. Nix	Chairman of the Building Fund
	F. L. Pearson	Architect of the Cathedral
	* W. G. Sandercock	Kea
	* H. C. Harris	Kea
	* P. A. Harefoot	Kea
Front Row. (l. to r.)	* W. P. Trestain	Kenwyn
	* E. C. Freund	Kenwyn
	N. M. Smeath	Captain
	Rev. M. Kelly	Master, Devon Guild of Bellringers
	J. C. Daubuz	Kea
	J. W. Taylor	Bell Founder. Loughborough
	* T. Sweet	Fowey
	* W. Slade	Fowey

Those marked (*) were the actual bellringers of the Cornish band at the inauguration. Other teams were made up of ringers from all parts of the West Country. The photograph also includes Frank Pearson, the architect, J. W. Taylor the Bell Founder and J. Daubuz an indefatigable worker for the cathedral and a benefactor.

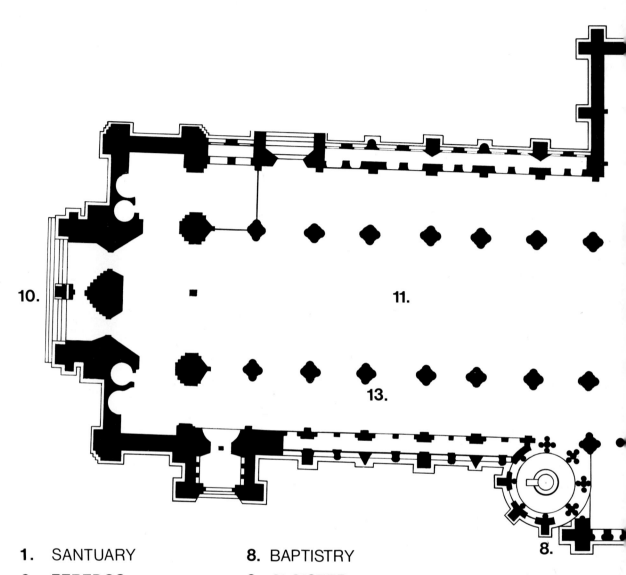

1. SANTUARY
2. REREDOS
3. BISHOP'S THRONE
4. CHOIR
5. PULPIT
6. ST. MARY'S AISLE
7. SOUTH PORCH

8. BAPTISTRY
9. CLOISTER
10. WEST PORCH
11. NAVE
12. FOUNDATION STONE
13. MEMORIAL STONE
14. STEPS TO CRYPT

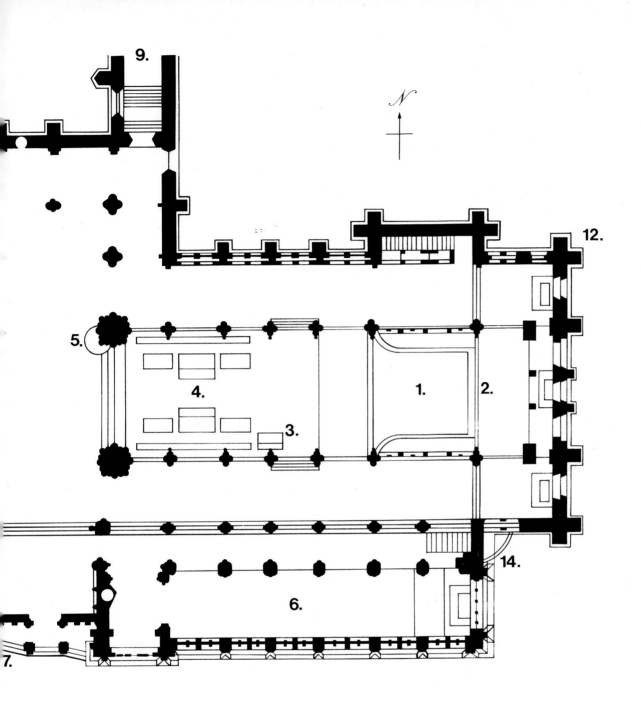

OVERALL LENGTH:	300 FEET	NAVE LENGTH: 131 FEET
OVERALL WIDTH:	62 FEET	HEIGHT OF CENTRAL TOWER: 244 FEET
TRANSEPT LENGTH:	109 FEET	HEIGHT OF WESTERN TOWERS: 200 FEET
TRANSEPT WIDTH:	58 FEET	

The cathedral, rich though it was in architecture, would have been but an empty shell had it not been furnished. The bishop, naturally, hoped that the interior would reflect the perfection of the building and he had the bright idea of appealing to the ladies of the diocese to undertake to raise the money required. On August 19th 1884, Bishop Wilkinson called them to a meeting in the temporary cathedral and 160 attended. They formed a committee with Miss Selina Thornton as secretary, and were divided into twelve divisions according to the rural deaneries. The demanding work of the general secretary was soon taken over by Mrs. Tremayne of Carclew (whose husband Arthur Tremayne was one of the survivors of the ill fated Charge of the Light Brigade) and under her leadership great efforts were made. Many functions were held, many appeals made and the poorest folk felt slighted if they were not asked to give to contribute something to the glorification of 'their' cathedral.

In a few months over £15,000 was raised and a tour of the building will reveal how great a result they achieved and few cathedrals can boast a finer set of church plate with every other item of the furnishing equally fine. The photograph, above, was probably taken about 1911 and shows a great gathering of those ladies, with the Bishop, outside the cathedral at a celebration of the culmination of their work. There is one other clergyman somewhat lost in the crowd and a lad with a chemist's bag probably dispensing aspirins!!

*During the building of the
choir, the especially designed
organ loft is seen being
prepared for the installation of
the instrument.*

*The organ as built and fitted
by Henry Willis in 1887 with
the console on the right and
some frontal pipes not installed.*

The 'Willis' Organ

PEDAL

1. Double Open Diapason 32ft
2. Open Diapason 16ft
3. Violone 16ft
4. Bourdon 16ft
5. Octave 8ft
6. Violoncello 8ft
7. Ophicleide 16ft
(6 Adjustable Pistons)

GREAT

8. Double Diapason 16ft
9. Open Diapason 8ft
10. Open Diapason 8ft
11. Clarabel 8ft
12. Principal 4ft
13. Flute Harmonique 4ft
14. Twelfth 2.2/3ft
15. Fifteenth 2ft
16. Mixture 17-19-22
17. Double Trumpet 16ft
18. Tromba 8ft
19. Clarion 4ft
(6 Adjustable Pistons)

SWELL

20. Geigen Principal 16ft
21. Open Diapason 8ft
22. Lieblich Gedackt 8ft
23. Echo Gamba 8ft
24. Vox Angelica 8ft
25. Geigen Principal 4ft
26. Flageolet 2ft
27. Mixture 17-19-22
28. Hautboy 8ft
29. Vox Humana 8ft
30. Contro Fagetto 16ft
31. Cornopean 8ft
32. Clarion 4ft
(6 Adjustable Pistons)

CHOIR

33. Gamba 8ft
34. Hohl Flote 8ft
35. Lieblich Gedackt 8ft
36. Dulciana 8ft
37. Gemshorn 4ft
38. Lieblich Flote 4ft
39. Piccolo 2ft
40. Corno di Bassetto 8ft
(4 Pistons)

SOLO

41. Flute Harmonique 8ft
42. Concert Flute 4ft
43. Orchestral Oboe 8ft
44. Clarinet 8ft
45. Tuba 8ft
(4 Pistons)

COUPLERS

I Great to Pedal
II Swell to Pedal
III Swell to Pedal 4
IV Solo to Pedal
V Solo to Pedal 4
VI Choir to Pedal
VII Swell to Great
VIII Swell to Great 4
IX Swell to Great 16
X Choir to Great
XI Solo to Great
XII Octave Swell
XIII Sub Octave Swell
XIV Swell to Choir
XV Solo to Choir
XVI Solo Octave
XVII Great & Pedal Combinations coupled

The detached console, installed in 1963, when the organ was cleaned and overhauled. This is situated over the south choir aisle and reached from there by a winding stairway.

The organ, after 1903, with the extra non-speaking frontal pipes added. These were in the original design but were left until the instrument was cleaned following the completion of the building work for the nave.

When it was decided to incorporate part of the old church into the fabric of the cathedral, Bishop Benson was not in favour of this 'tinkering up of old stones' as he put it. It is true that Mr. Pearson had plenty of problems as the old aisle wall was 9½″ out of the perpendicular and so much stone needed replacement that virtual rebuilding was necessary.

In this photograph, taken in 1890, the fine east window is seen also the old Byfield organ, dating from 1750. In the restoration of 1961, the roof was replastered on traditional lines drawing attention to the fine carved ribs and wall plates of the old roof which had been carefully replaced on rebuilding. Theoretically it would be possible to remove the aisle and bell tower and the cathedral would still be intact but this happy blend gives a young cathedral some history going back over many centuries.

Moving up from St. Mary's aisle to the chancel, we see the small extra aisle, or ambulatory, which created the support and took the thrust of the outer wall of the choir. The forest of columns and ascending effect are noticeable and this photograph was taken before the nave was completed and some worshippers were given seats in the aisles.

A general view of the chancel with the choir stalls, the great organ, the pulpit, reredos and the altar.

The magnificent Reredos, or screen, carved in stone depicting scenes from the scriptures. The architect originally intended this to be of a greater height but it was not completed due to economic necessity.

Looking down the length of the cathedral, from the sanctuary, across the splendid carved stalls of the choir, in the twenties, with the sounding board over the pulpit. The return stalls and bases of the intended choir screen are seen in place but this feature was not proceeded with and the bases removed in 1961 and the return stalls shortened. This viewpoint again gives an indication of the deviation in the line of the nave and chancel.

The Bishop's chair, or 'cathedra', from which the word cathedral is derived, is situated to the east of the choir stalls and is richly carved in Burmese teak. This photograph was taken in 1887, at the completion of the choir and the bishops crests have not been added. It shows the temporary gallery erected over the only partially built two bays of the nave and the canon's stalls have not been added as they would have screened off much of the congregation, who for many years, had to be seated in the choir aisles before they could be accommodated in the nave.

The magnificent pulpit, carved in Hopton Wood stone, situated at one of the four great columns of the crossing, below the tower. In lofty vaulted buildings with many corners and passages, there is usually an acoustic problem and here the preacher was almost inaudible any distance away. An attempt was made to overcome this by fitting a sounding board at an angle over this pulpit, which produced some improvement but the advent of public address systems has been a boon.

The magnificent lectern, fashioned in brass, a fine example of the Victorian panel beaters art. It was given to the cathedral by Miss Harriet Lanyon, of Truro, whose father had been one of Nelsons sailing masters. It was probably one of the very first offerings for the new edifice and was set for a time in old St. Mary's so it must be well nigh 100 years old.

The vista from the south entrance, looking over the crossing to the north transept where are contained the memorials, mostly removed from the old church, with that of the Robartes family prominent.

Looking down into the south transept from the triforium, this demonstrates the great height at the crossing and also shows the rose window over the south porch. The south transept has only two bays, because of the narrow street, whereas there are three in the northern arm.

The Baptistry, one of the most attractive features of the church interior, with its circular formation contrasting with the regular lines of the rest of the building. It was dedicated to Henry Martyn, a Truro Missionary, who died abroad of fever. The font is of red porphry and the cover of oak.

Opposite page

The nave, from the west door, with its splendid plain vaulting leading naturally to the more decorated treatment of the chancel. The deviation in the ground plan can be noticed from this angle.

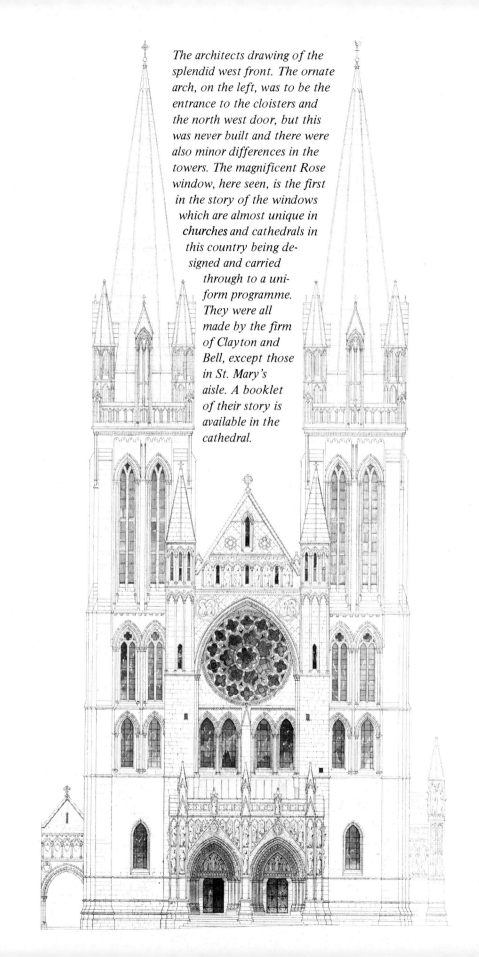

The architects drawing of the splendid west front. The ornate arch, on the left, was to be the entrance to the cloisters and the north west door, but this was never built and there were also minor differences in the towers. The magnificent Rose window, here seen, is the first in the story of the windows which are almost unique in churches and cathedrals in this country being designed and carried through to a uniform programme. They were all made by the firm of Clayton and Bell, except those in St. Mary's aisle. A booklet of their story is available in the cathedral.

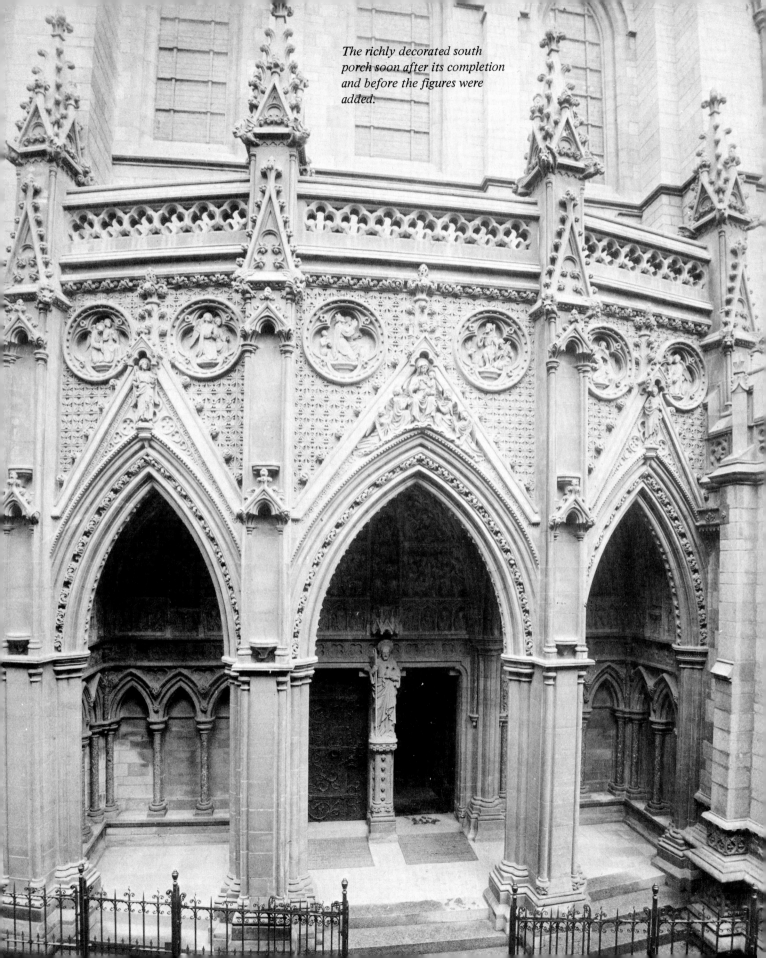

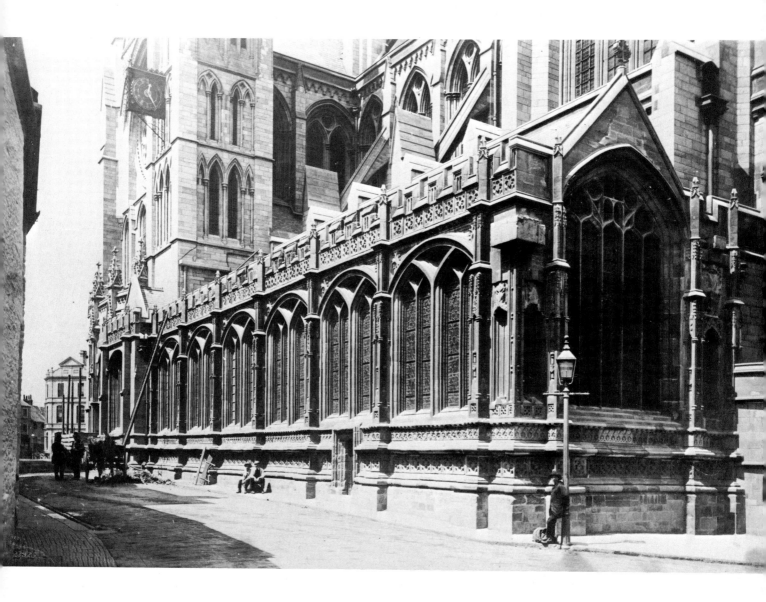

The clock mechanism was presented to the old church in 1851 and installed in the steeple together with the chiming apparatus. This was removed at the demolition and later fitted to the new campanile. This bell tower and the retained St. Mary's aisle now constitute the official parish church of Truro. The 130 ft. tower is prominent with its sheath of green Cornish copper and this was to have been fitted on all roofs but the expense proved too great.

As can be seen in the above photograph, the clock had a new face (presented by Canon Wise of Ladock) jutting out from the tower on struts but the action of wind force and corrosion made it unsafe and it was removed and stored. The clock has continued to function, faceless, only passing its time to the populace at each quarter hour when it chimes. Heavy electrical storms, in the summer of 1975, affected the winding motors and the clock was out of action for some months.

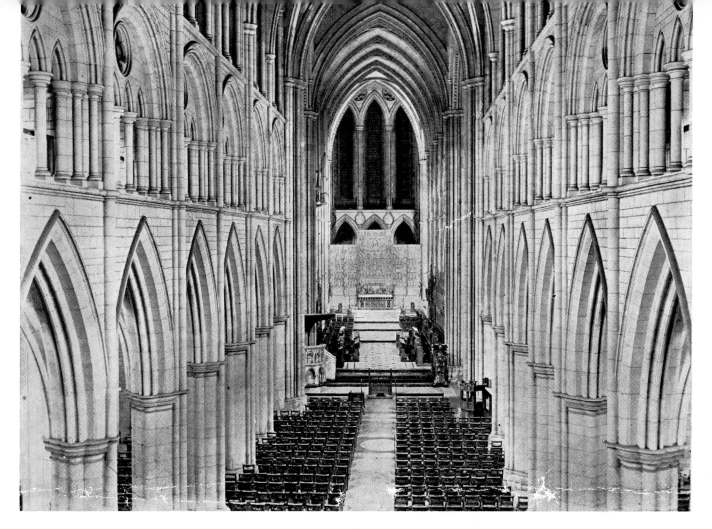

When the cathedral was completed it was illuminated by gas as electricity was not of course available. In the twenties it was decided to install electric lighting and the Falmouth firm of J.H. Deeble and Son, won the contract with a scheme prepared by G.E.C. of London. To enable work to be carried out quickly and without the need of cumbersome scaffolding, the firm designed a movable platform. This was constructed of heavy timber frame, mounted on 6″ castors, and carried two 35 ft. extending ladders. It was more than a little nerve racking when working at the top but it facilitated the work, and the equipment could be moved out of the way at the end of each day.

The main fuses and switchgear were installed in the north transept wall and still are, but there is now an illuminated wiring diagram to show the items switched in. All the main cables were specially woven and carried in steel conduits with lead casing down to the fitments. Modern metal box channelling now carries the cables through the triforium and many are very long as it is impossible to go over or under the nave, and they have to be carried around the end of the church. The original lighting was provided by 200 watt screwed bulbs in flood light reflectors and the reredos and altar was illuminated by 12 ft. strip lights concealed behind the last columns of the sanctuary. Later installations have made use of spotlights which highlight the architecture and the organ has been improved by electro-pneumatic operation. Some of the old gas lighting had metal tubes from the roof over 60 ft. in length and when these were removed they were purchased by a farmer who used them for his irrigation scheme.

In the thirties the first public address system was installed and this has been improved over the years. There are now microphones at the altar, pulpit, lectern and over the choir and these are relayed to the nave and other parts of the cathedral which has contributed to the congregation entering more fully in the service.

On May 20th 1967, the last addition to the cathedral was made when the splendid chapter house was opened. The scene, above, is of the occasion and the Lord Bishop and the Dean escort The Hon. Hilaria St. Aubyn and the Hon. Mrs. John Parker daughters of the Lord St. Levan in whose memory they have presented the building. They are also grandaughters of the Earl of Mount Edgcumbe who was the chairman of the original building committee and who played a great part in the success of the operation. Below, the Mayor of Truro, followed by those of other Cornish Boroughs, enter the building after the ceremony.

The completed chapter house with its modern, though ecclesiastical appearance. The raised base is intended to bring it to the same height as the cathedral floor.

By this new building the Dean and Chapter have now a splendid meeting place and it has enabled other bodies, both religious and secular to make use of the cathedral environment as a centre. This has widened the scope of the church's influence and is making it a community as well as a religious focal point.

The old grammar school, with which the church had long associations, was in financial difficulties at the end of the last century. The cathedral body played a leading role in trying to raise money and influenced their own bene-factor, Mrs. Hawkins of Trewithen, to donate £500 with more if others contributed. Despite this help the school was still not paying it's way and eventually the Dean and Chapter took over complete control and it became known as the Truro Cathedral Grammar School with later the 'grammar' being dropped altogether.

A new building was required and the cathedral architect, Frank Pearson, was asked to prepare a design to be erected in the precincts and to form a part of the cathedral buildings. (See painting on page 5). Mrs. Hawkins came for-ward with the necessary finance and she performed the ceremony of laying the foundation stone on October 21st 1908. The connection to the cathedral was never made and the unfinished walls can still be seen. Free school scholar-ships were given to choristers and during the early part of the 1939-45 war the boys of the choir of St. Paul's, London, were evacuated to Truro and they joined in the curriculum. In later years the school has acquired new buildings at Kenwyn and has gradually moved away from the close leaving the old structure to be used as offices by the local council.

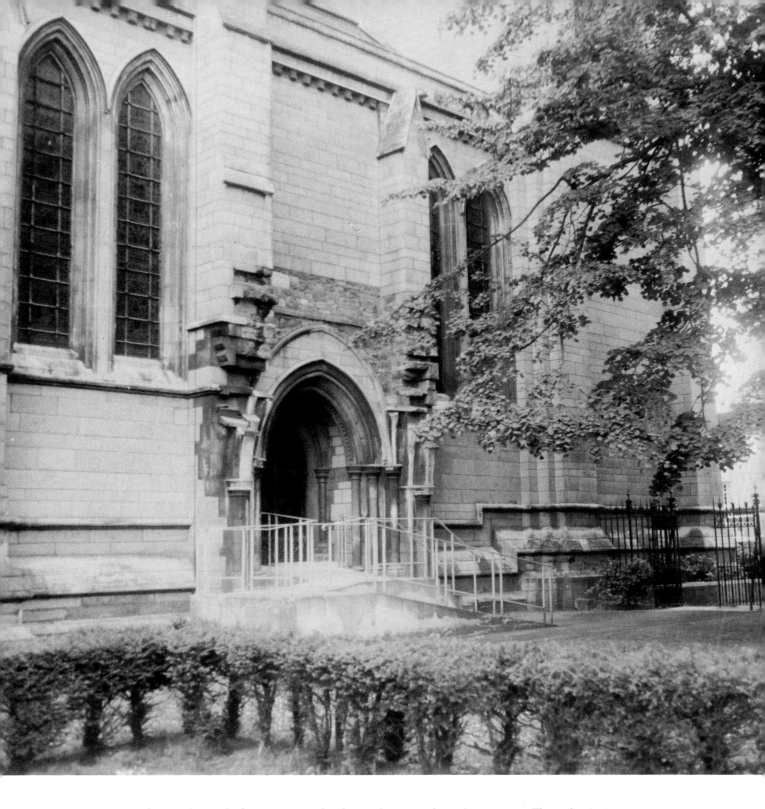

The north west door, which opens on to the close, is here seen from the precincts. The unfinished surround is evident and this was intended to become part of the cloisters with a decorated arch giving an entrance from the roadway at the west end. This porch has been fitted with a ramp to allow disabled persons to enter the cathedral.

Weathering of the Bath stone caused some portions to crumble and fall, during the sixties. Repairs were made and some reconstituted stone was used. During work on the main steeple, the weather vane was removed and it is here being replaced by a naval helicopter from the Culdrose Air Station, Helston.

Still standing, some eighty years after its removal from Truro, the gothic design of the windows marks out the old wooden building that served as Cornwall's cathedral between 1880 and 1887. Now mounted on a brick base it acts as a store in Drump Road, Redruth.

ACKNOWLEDGEMENTS

The Very Reverent Henry Morgan Lloyd, D.S.O., M.B.E., M.A., Dean of the Cathedral. Help and Guidance.
John Phillips, A.R.I.B.A., Consultant Architect to the cathedral. Technical Advice.
Canon H. Miles Brown, Diocesan Historian. Historical Advice.
Mrs. W. J. Coode, Falmouth. Photographs from the Daubauz collection.
Royal Institute of Cornwall, Truro. Photographs and old newspapers.
County Records Office, Truro. Photographs and old Records.
Jack Major, Camborne. Old books for reference.
Colin Nunn, Falmouth. Old print of St. Mary's.
Alan Carveth, Truro. Photographs and drawing.
Robin Reynolds, Chelmsford. Colour photograph of the cathedra.
The Commanding Officer, R.N.A.S. Culdrose. Aerial photographs.
Derek Godfrey, Mitchell. Old negative of Cathedral.
Western Morning News, Plymouth. Photographs of Chapter ceremony.
John Miles, Falmouth. Old photograph copying.
Bishop Philpotts Library, Truro. Access to Diocesan Gazettes.

BIBLIOGRAPHY

The Bishopric of Truro.	Donaldson. 1902
The Cornish See and Cathedral.	Heard. 1887
Cathedral Spires.	Rowe. 1947
Diocesan Gazette	Various Years
West Briton Newspaper.	Various Years
Royal Cornwall Gazette Newspaper	Various Years
The Illustrated London News.	1887
The Graphic	1880

ISBNO 0 9502825 2 9

Published by	GLASNEY PRESS, Falmouth.
Designed by	Oxford Publishing Co. Oxford.
Printed by	B.H. Blackwell Ltd. in the City of Oxford.
Artwork by	Terence Fisher Barham, London.

GLASNEY   PRESS
Publishers of Illustrated Histories.